A STRATEGY OF PEACE

JFK's American University Speech

With Commentary by Michio Kushi,
Edward Esko, Bill Tara, John Liebmann,
Dennis Kucinich, & Alex Jack

Amberwaves Press

A Strategy of Peace
JFK's American University Speech
© 2018 by individual contributors

ISBN–13–978-1981466207
ISBN-10– 1981466207

Published by Amber Waves Press
Box 487, Becket MA 01223
413-623-0012

Amberwavesofgrain.com
Makropedia.com
Macrobioticsummerconference.com
Misohappyshow.com
Culinarymedicine.com

Printed in the U.S.A.

"So, let us not be blind to our differences—but let us also direct attention to our common interests and to the means by which those differences can be resolved. And if we cannot end now our differences, at least we can help make the world safe for diversity. For, in the final analysis, our most basic common link is that we all inhabit this small planet. We all breathe the same air. We all cherish our children's future. And we are all mortal."
—John F. Kennedy

"We are not only able to feed ourselves taking into account our lands, water resources–Russia is able to become the largest world supplier of healthy, ecologically clean and high-quality food."
—Vladimir Putin

"As people living on the planet at this time, we can overcome global crisis by taking responsibility for our diets, our ways of life, and our ways of thinking. It is an urgent task for all of us to reflect upon our daily life, and to share with and inspire those who surround us in our communities, our countries, as well as on the entire planet."
—Michio Kushi

Contents

ALEX JACK
Preface

Like Lao Tzu, the ancient Chinese sage and author of the *Tao Te Ching*, John F. Kennedy's words intuitively grasped the dynamic play of complementary opposites, or yin and yang:

- Change is the law of life. And those who look only to the past or present are certain to miss the future

- The greater our knowledge increases, the more our ignorance unfolds

- Too often we... enjoy the comfort of opinion without the discomfort of thought

- Physical fitness is not only one of the most important keys to a healthy body, it is the basis of dynamic and creative intellectual activity

- If more politicians knew poetry, and more poets knew politics, I am convinced the world would be a little better place in which to live

- Let us never negotiate out of fear. But let us never fear to negotiate

- Mankind must put an end to war before war puts an end to mankind

- Those who make peaceful revolution impossible will make violent revolution inevitable

- We are not here to curse the darkness, but to light the candle that can guide us through that darkness to a safe and sane future

- Ask not what your country can do for you—ask what you can do for your country

- We celebrate the past to awaken the future

President Kennedy's American University Speech on peace was one of the great orations in American history. It led to the Partial Nuclear Test-Ban Treaty—the first thaw in the Cold War and the first successful international effort to slow the nuclear arms race.

While the Cold War has been over for a generation, there are many parallels today. As in the early 1960s, the threat of nuclear war (in Korea now compared to Cuba then) has galvanized renewed interest in arms control, including the recent summit between President Donald Trump and Chairman Kim Jong-un of North Korea. The practical results of their meeting remain to be seen.

The rise of an unaccountable executive and clandestine operatives (shadowy Russian contacts and hackers now vs. CIA agents and assets then) also mirrors the late Eisenhower years, early Kennedy administration, and the Bay of Pigs fiasco.

A major catalyst for this volume was James W. Douglass's book *JFK and the Unspeakable: Why He Died and Why It Matters* that documents the extraordinary, largely unknown turn toward peace by Kennedy—and Premier Khrushchev—after the Cuban Missile Crisis and the inside story of how the military and intelligence agencies in the U.S. brought the president down.

The universal goal of the international macrobiotic community has long been One Peaceful World. After educator Michio Kushi passed away, the Michio Kushi Peace Prize was established to honor his memory. The recipients were selected on the basis of their lifetime contribution to health, peace, and sustainability: Shizuko Yamamoto (2015), Dennis Kucinich (2016), Neal Barnard, M.D. (2017), and Martha Clayton Cottrell, M.D (2018).

In this volume, several leading macrobiotic teachers and peace promoters discuss JFK's legacy and its relevance today. We hope Kennedy's stirring words and bold deeds—the Peace Corps, the peaceful exploration of outer space, and the nuclear test ban treaty—will inspire future generations to awaken to humanity's universal dream of health and peace and ask not what their planet can do for them, but what they can do for their planet.

Alex Jack is president of Planetary Health, Inc. and author of One Peaceful World *(with Michio Kushi),* The One Peaceful World Cookbook *(with Sachi Kato), and* The Circle of the Dance: Achilles's Shield, Odysseus's Oar, Calypso's Axe, and the New Golden Age. *He lives in the Berkshires.*

JOHN F. KENNEDY
Address at American University
Washington, D.C.
June 10, 1963

President Anderson, members of the faculty, board of trustees, distinguished guests, my old colleague, Senator Bob Byrd, who has earned his degree through many years of attending night law school while I am earning mine in the next 30 minutes, ladies and gentlemen:

It is with great pride that I participate in this ceremony of the American University, sponsored by the Methodist Church, founded by Bishop John Fletcher Hurst, and first opened by President Woodrow Wilson in 1914. This is a young and growing university, but it has already fulfilled Bishop Hurst's enlightened hope for the study of history and public affairs in a city devoted to the making of history and to the conduct of the public's business. By sponsoring this institution of higher learning for all who wish to learn, whatever their color or their creed, the Methodists of this area and the Nation deserve the Nation's thanks, and I commend all those who are today graduating.

Professor Woodrow Wilson once said that every man sent out from a university should be a man of his nation as well as a man of his time, and I am confident that the men and women who carry the honor of graduating from this institution will continue to give from their lives, from their talents, a high measure of public service and public support.

"There are few earthly things more beautiful than a university," wrote John Masefield, in his tribute to English universities—and his words are equally true today. He did not refer to spires and towers, to campus greens and ivied walls. He admired the splendid beauty of the university, he said, because it was "a place where those who hate ignorance may strive to know, where those who perceive truth may strive to make others see."

I have, therefore, chosen this time and this place to discuss a topic on which ignorance too often abounds and the truth is too rarely perceived—yet it is the most important topic on earth: world peace.

What kind of peace do I mean? What kind of peace do we seek? Not a Pax Americana enforced on the world by American weapons of war. Not the peace of the grave or the security of the slave. I am talking about genuine peace, the kind of peace that makes life on earth worth living, the kind that enables men and nations to grow and to hope and to build a better life for their children—not merely peace for Americans but peace for all men and women—not merely peace in our time but peace for all time.

I speak of peace because of the new face of war. Total war makes no sense in an age when great powers can maintain large and relatively invulnerable nuclear forces and refuse to surrender without resort to those forces. It makes no sense in an age when a single nuclear weapon contains almost ten times the explosive force delivered by all of the allied air forces in the Second World War. It makes no sense in an age when the deadly poisons produced by a nuclear exchange would be carried by wind and water and soil and seed to the far corners of the globe and to generations yet unborn.

Today the expenditure of billions of dollars every year on weapons acquired for the purpose of making sure we never need to use them is essential to keeping the peace. But surely the acquisition of such idle stockpiles—which can only destroy and never create—is not the only, much less the most efficient, means of assuring peace.

I speak of peace, therefore, as the necessary rational end of rational men. I realize that the pursuit of peace is not as dramatic as the pursuit of war—and frequently the words of the pursuer fall on deaf ears. But we have no more urgent task.

Some say that it is useless to speak of world peace or world law or world disarmament-and that it will be useless until the leaders of the Soviet Union adopt a more enlightened attitude. I hope they do. I believe we can help them do it. But I also believe that we must reexamine our own attitude—as individuals and as a Nation—for our attitude is as essential as theirs. And every graduate of this school, every thoughtful citizen who despairs of war and wishes to bring peace, should begin by looking inward—by examining his own attitude toward the possibilities of peace, toward the Soviet Union, toward the course of the cold war and toward freedom and peace here at home.

First: Let us examine our attitude toward peace itself. Too many of us think it is impossible. Too many think it unreal. But that is a dangerous, defeatist belief. It leads to the conclusion that war is inevitable—that mankind is doomed—that we are gripped by forces we cannot control.

We need not accept that view. Our problems are manmade—therefore, they can be solved by man. And man can be as big as he wants. No problem of human destiny is beyond human beings. Man's reason and spirit have often solved the seemingly unsolvable—and we believe they can do it again.

I am not referring to the absolute, infinite concept of universal peace and good will of which some fantasies and fanatics dream. I do not deny the value of hopes and dreams but we merely invite discouragement and incredulity by making that our only and immediate goal.

Let us focus instead on a more practical, more attainable peace—based not on a sudden revolution in human nature but on a gradual evolution in human institutions—on a series of concrete actions and effective agreements which are in the interest of all concerned. There is no single, simple key to this peace--no grand or magic formula to be adopted by one or two powers. Genuine peace must be the product of many nations, the sum of many acts. It must be dynamic, not static, changing to meet the challenge of each new generation. For peace is a process—a way of solving problems.

With such a peace, there will still be quarrels and conflicting interests, as there are within families and nations. World peace, like community peace, does not require that each man love his neighbor—it requires only that they live together in mutual tolerance, submitting their disputes to a just and peaceful settlement. And history teaches us that enmities between nations, as between individuals, do not last forever. However fixed our likes and dislikes may seem, the tide of time and events will often bring surprising changes in the relations between nations and neighbors.

So let us persevere. Peace need not be impracticable, and war need not be inevitable. By defining our goal more clearly, by making it seem more manageable and less remote, we can help all peoples to see it, to draw hope from it, and to move irresistibly toward it.

Second: Let us reexamine our attitude toward the Soviet Union. It is discouraging to think that their leaders may actually believe what their propagandists write. It is discouraging to read a recent authoritative Soviet text on Military Strategy and find, on page after page, wholly baseless and incredible claims—such as the allegation that "American imperialist circles are preparing to unleash different types of wars ... that there is a very real threat of a preventive war being unleashed by American imperialists against the Soviet Union ... [and that] the political aims of the American imperialists are to enslave economically and politically the European and other capitalist countries... [and] to achieve world domination ... by means of aggressive wars."

Truly, as it was written long ago: "The wicked flee when no man pursueth." Yet it is sad to read these Soviet statements—to realize the extent of the gulf between us. But it is also a warning—a warning to the American people not to fall into the same trap as the Soviets, not to see only a distorted and desperate view of the other side, not to see conflict as inevitable, accommodation as impossible, and communication as nothing more than an exchange of threats.

No government or social system is so evil that its people must be considered as lacking in virtue. As Americans, we find communism profoundly repugnant as a negation of personal freedom and dignity. But we can still hail the Russian people for their many achievements—in science and space, in economic and industrial growth, in culture and in acts of courage.

Among the many traits the peoples of our two countries have in common, none is stronger than our mutual abhorrence of war. Almost unique, among the major world powers, we have never been at war with each other. And no nation in the history of battle ever suffered more than the Soviet Union suffered in the course of the Second World War. At least 20 million lost their lives. Countless millions of homes and farms were burned or sacked. A third of the nation's territory, including nearly two thirds of its industrial base, was turned into a wasteland—a loss equivalent to the devastation of this country east of Chicago.

Today, should total war ever break out again—no matter how—our two countries would become the primary targets. It is an ironic but accurate fact that the two strongest powers are the two in the most danger of devastation. All we have built, all we have worked for, would be destroyed in the first 24 hours. And even in the cold war, which brings burdens and dangers to so many countries, including this Nation's closest allies—our two countries bear the heaviest burdens. For we are both devoting massive sums of money to weapons that could be better devoted to combating ignorance, poverty, and disease. We are both caught up in a vicious and dangerous cycle in which suspicion on one side breeds suspicion on the other, and new weapons beget counter-weapons.

In short, both the United States and its allies, and the Soviet Union and its allies, have a mutually deep interest in a just and genuine peace and in halting the arms race. Agreements to this end are in the interests of the Soviet

Union as well as ours—and even the most hostile nations can be relied upon to accept and keep those treaty obligations, and only those treaty obligations, which are in their own interest.

So, let us not be blind to our differences-but let us also direct attention to our common interests and to the means by which those differences can be resolved. And if we cannot end now our differences, at least we can help make the world safe for diversity. For, in the final analysis, our most basic common link is that we all inhabit this small planet. We all breathe the same air. We all cherish our children's future. And we are all mortal.

Third: Let us reexamine our attitude toward the cold war, remembering that we are not engaged in a debate, seeking to pile up debating points. We are not here distributing blame or pointing the finger of judgment. We must deal with the world as it is, and not as it might have been had the history of the last 18 years been different.

We must, therefore, persevere in the search for peace in the hope that constructive changes within the Communist bloc might bring within reach solutions which now seem beyond us. We must conduct our affairs in such a way that it becomes in the Communists' interest to agree on a genuine peace. Above all, while defending our own vital interests, nuclear powers must avert those confrontations which bring an adversary to a choice of either a humiliating retreat or a nuclear war. To adopt that kind of course in the nuclear age would be evidence only of the bankruptcy of our policy-or of a collective death-wish for the world.

To secure these ends, America's weapons are nonprovocative, carefully controlled, designed to deter, and capable of selective use. Our military forces are committed to peace and disciplined in self-restraint. Our diplomats are instructed to avoid unnecessary irritants and purely rhetorical hostility.

For we can seek a relaxation of tensions without relaxing our guard. And, for our part, we do not need to use threats to prove that we are resolute. We do not need to jam foreign broadcasts out of fear our faith will be eroded. We are unwilling to impose our system on any unwilling people—but we are willing and able to engage in peaceful competition with any people on earth.

Meanwhile, we seek to strengthen the United Nations, to help solve its financial problems, to make it a more effective instrument for peace, to develop it into a genuine world security system—a system capable of resolving disputes on the basis of law, of insuring the security of the large and the small, and of creating conditions under which arms can finally be abolished.

At the same time we seek to keep peace inside the non-Communist world, where many nations, all of them our friends, are divided over issues which weaken Western unity, which invite Communist intervention or which threaten to erupt into war. Our efforts in West New Guinea, in the Congo, in the Middle East, and in the Indian subcontinent, have been persistent and patient despite criticism from both sides. We have also tried to set an example for others—by seeking to adjust small but significant differences with our own closest neighbors in Mexico and in Canada. Speaking of other nations, I wish to make one point clear. We are bound to many nations by alliances. Those alliances exist because our concern and theirs substantially overlap. Our commitment to defend Western Europe and West Berlin, for example, stands undiminished because of the identify of our vital interests. The United States will make no deal with the Soviet Union at the expense of other nations and other peoples, not merely because they are our partners, but also because their interests and ours converge.

Our interests converge, however, not only in defending the frontiers of freedom, but in pursuing the paths of peace. It is our hope—and the purpose of allied policies—to convince the Soviet Union that she, too, should let each nation choose its own future, so long as that choice does not interfere with the choices of others. The Communist drive to impose their political and economic system on others is the primary cause of world tension today. For there can be no doubt that, if all nations could refrain from interfering in the self-determination of others, the peace would be much more assured.

This will require a new effort to achieve world law--a new context for world discussions. It will require increased understanding between the Soviets and ourselves. And increased understanding will require increased contact and communication. One step in this direction is the proposed arrangement for a direct line between Moscow and Washington, to avoid on each side the dangerous delays, misunderstandings, and misreadings of the other's actions which might occur at a time of crisis.

We have also been talking in Geneva about other first-step measures of arms control, designed to limit the intensity of the arms race and to reduce the risks of accidental war. Our primary long-range interest in Geneva, however, is general and complete disarmament—designed to take place by stages, permitting parallel political developments to build the new institutions of peace which would take the place of arms.

The pursuit of disarmament has been an effort of of this Government since the 1920s. It has been urgently sought by the past three administrations. And however dim the prospects may be today, we intend to continue this effort—to continue it in order that all countries, including our own, can better grasp what the problems and possibilities of disarmament are.

The one major area of these negotiations where the end is in sight, yet where a fresh start is badly needed, is in a treaty to outlaw nuclear tests. The conclusion of such a treaty, so near and yet so far, would check the spiraling arms race in one of its most dangerous areas. It would place the nuclear powers in a position to deal more effectively with one of the greatest hazards which man faces in 1963, the further spread of nuclear arms. It would increase our security—it would decrease the prospects of war. Surely this goal is sufficiently important to require our steady pursuit, yielding neither to the temptation to give up the whole effort nor the temptation to give up our insistence on vital and responsible safeguards.

I am taking this opportunity, therefore, to announce two important decisions in this regard.

First: Chairman Khrushchev, Prime Minister Macmillan, and I have agreed that high-level discussions will shortly begin in Moscow looking toward early agreement on a comprehensive test ban treaty. Our hopes must be tempered with the caution of history—but with our hopes go the hopes of all mankind.

Second: To make clear our good faith and solemn convictions on the matter, I now declare that the United States does not propose to conduct nuclear tests in the atmosphere so long as other states do not do so. We will not be the first to resume. Such a declaration is no substitute for a formal binding treaty, but I hope it will help us achieve one. Nor would such a treaty be a substitute for disarmament, but I hope it will help us achieve it.

Finally, my fellow Americans, let us examine our attitude toward peace and freedom here at home. The quality and spirit of our own society must justify and support our efforts abroad. We must show it in the dedication of our own lives—as many of you who are graduating today will have a unique opportunity to do, by serving without pay in the Peace Corps abroad or in the proposed National Service Corps here at home.

But wherever we are, we must all, in our daily lives, live up to the age-old faith that peace and freedom walk together. In too many of our cities today, the peace is not secure because freedom is incomplete.

It is the responsibility of the executive branch at all levels of government—local, State, and National--to provide and protect that freedom for all of our citizens by all means within their authority. It is the responsibility of the legislative branch at all levels, wherever that authority is not now adequate, to make it adequate. And it is the responsibility of all citizens in all sections of this country to respect the rights of all others and to respect the law of the land.

All this is not unrelated to world peace. "When a man's ways please the Lord," the Scriptures tell us, "he maketh even his enemies to be at peace with him." And is not peace, in the last analysis, basically a matter of human rights—the right to live out our lives without fear of devastation-the right to breathe air as nature provided it—the right of future generations to a healthy existence?

While we proceed to safeguard our national interests, let us also safeguard human interests. And the elimination of war and arms is clearly in the interest of both. No treaty, however much it may be to the advantage of all, however tightly it may be worded, can provide absolute security against the risks of deception and evasion. But it can—if it is sufficiently effective in its enforcement and if it is sufficiently in the interests of its signers—offer far more security and far fewer risks than an unabated, uncontrolled, unpredictable arms race.

The United States, as the world knows, will never start a war. We do not want a war. We do not now expect a war. This generation of Americans has already had enough—more than enough—of war and hate and oppression. We shall be prepared if others wish it. We shall be alert to try to stop it. But we shall also do our part to build a world of peace where the weak are safe and the strong are just. We are not helpless before that task or hopeless of its success. Confident and unafraid, we labor on—not toward a strategy of annihilation but toward a strategy of peace.

Note: The President spoke at the John M. Reeves Athletic Field on the campus of American University after being awarded an honorary degree of doctor of laws. In his opening words he referred to Hurst R. Anderson, president of the university, and Robert C. Byrd, U.S. Senator from West Virginia.

MICHIO KUSHI
Message to the United Nations
International Macrobiotic Society
New York, New York
April 25, 1986

Throughout the world, biological, psychological, and spiritual degeneration is prevailing. This degeneration is the basis for international conflicts that pose serious obstacles to the quest for one peaceful world.

Our macrobiotic education has inspired the change in food patterns throughout the world toward a more natural and healthy direction. The natural food movement has reversed the modern decline in food quality.

Our education has also contributed to public awareness of individual and family responsibility; teaching that the real cause of sickness lies in our daily diet and way of life. Hundreds of thousands of people in America, Europe, and other regions of the world have recovered health and well being through our educational efforts conducted together with several hundred macrobiotic centers.

Over the past quarter century, we have demonstrated how to prevent and recover from heart disease, various types of cancer, and most recently, AIDS and immune deficiencies. In each of these areas, a large number of people have benefitted from macrobiotic education.

Research teams at Harvard, the Framingham Heart Study, Boston University, and Ghent University in Belgium, have documented the effectiveness of macrobiotics through ongoing studies.

Unfortunately, in spite of these efforts, there have also been some who were not able to recover their conditions, and to these people, we extend our heartfelt sympathy. Recently, we lost a member of the International Macrobiotic Society, Mr. Shigeaki Numata. He began the serious practice of macrobiotics in hopes of recovering from stomach cancer. Then, after his European trip, he began to weaken.

Even with the close cooperation of his family, macrobiotic friends, and medical doctors, he was not able to recover. We are all saddened by his passing and extend our deepest sympathy to his family, along with our prayers for his peaceful journey to the spiritual world.

We have encountered many people, who like Mr. Numata, were not able to recover from serious conditions. Yet, at the same time, we have also witnessed many inspiring recoveries from terminal illnesses.

It is important to remember that recovery from sickness depends on improving the quality of our environment, our way of life, and our civilization at large. One person may die, and other may live; but survival is not simply a problem for all of us as individuals, it is the most pressing concern of humanity today.

As people living on the planet at this time, we can overcome global crisis by taking responsibility for our diets, our ways of life, and our ways of thinking. It is an urgent task for all of us to reflect upon our daily life, and to share with and inspire those who surround us in our communities, our countries, as well as on the entire planet.

EDWARD ESKO
Address at the Macrobiotic Summer Conference
Becket, Massachusetts
August 2014

When President Kennedy delivered his famous "Peace" speech in 1963, the world crisis was less diverse than today. That was in the era before climate change, burgeoning world population, GMOs, mounting nuclear waste, massive dead zones in the world's oceans, and increased proliferation of nuclear weapons. Nuclear war was the primary and apparent threat to human existence. Of course, the problem of nuclear war is as urgent now as it was then, but it is increasingly a part of an interrelated spectrum of existential threats, some of which we will review in this presentation.

One of the most important milestones leading up to the current world crisis was the development of nitrogen fertilizer. Why was that important? What had been going on up to that time? Plants make protein from nitrogen. For centuries, farmers obtained nitrogen by composting, adding manure from animals, or alternating their crops. Certain bean crops, called legumes, have root structures that enable certain bacteria, known as nitrogen-fixing bacteria, to pull in and "fix" nitrogen from the atmosphere, forming natural fertilizer, which the plants can use.

However, these methods created a limit to the growth of human population. Up until 1900, the earth's population was approximately 1.6 billion.

Soon after that, engineers in Germany developed an energy-intensive method to extract nitrogen from the atmosphere, literally from thin air. Nitrogen is about 80% of the atmosphere. However it exists not as a single atom but as a molecule of two atoms of nitrogen, or N_2. These atoms are not identical. Like snowflakes, no two atoms or preatomic particles are. They occupy unique positions in time and space. They share configuration but are unique within that configuration. The atoms in the nitrogen molecule spin in opposite directions. Whenever polarized opposites combine, they are very difficult to separate. Haber and Bosch developed a method to separate the nitrogen atoms and produce ammonia, which is then used to manufacture nitrate fertilizer. Initially nitrate was used in high explosives and munitions. It was the main force behind the explosive power of World War II. After World War II the focus shifted toward fertilizer.

According to Wikipedia:

> "The Haber process now produces 450 million tons (440,000,000 long tons; 500,000,000 short tons) of nitrogen fertilizer per year, mostly in the form of anhydrous ammonia, ammonium nitrate, and urea. 3–5% of the world's natural gas production is consumed in the Haber process (~1–2% of the world's annual energy supply). In combination with pesticides, these fertilizers have quadrupled the productivity of agricultural land.
>
> "Due to its dramatic impact on the human ability to grow food, the Haber process served as

the 'detonator of the population explosion,' enabling the global population to increase from 1.6 billion in 1900 to today's 7 billion. Nearly 80% of the nitrogen found in human tissues originated from the Haber-Bosch process. Since nitrogen use efficiency is typically less than 50% our heavy use of industrial nitrogen fixation is disruptive to our biological habitat."

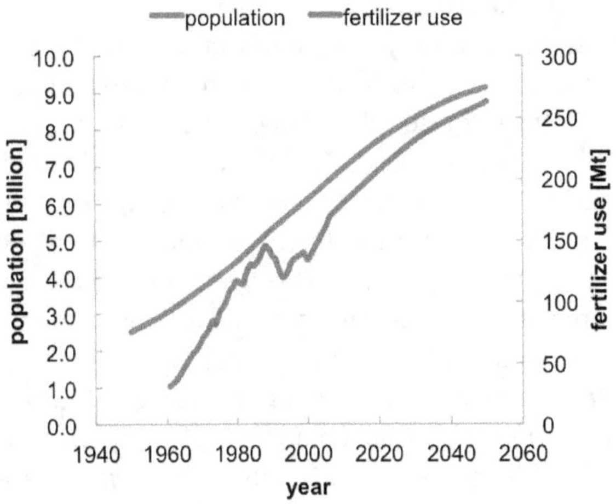

High yield varieties (HYV) of crops were developed to accept this fertilizer. They were developed through plant genetics. As a result, the production of wheat, corn, soy, and rice increased dramatically. Following that, world population exploded. The population went from 1.6 billion in 1900 to 7 billion today. This is an example of exponential growth, especially when we look at population trends over the past several centuries. Growth is very slow and incremental at the beginning but as that increase continues, growth suddenly becomes enormous. The skyrocketing curve resembles a hockey stick as it sharply escalates.

In America, the majority of the high yield soybeans and corn crops are not used for direct human consumption but are fed to livestock. The livestock industry became increasingly centralized.

Seventy percent of these crops are used to feed livestock. The diet became based on mass produced, factory farmed animal food. Animals are confined in highly artificial spaces in a system known as "confinement agriculture." What has that led to?

That system is highly inefficient. It takes thirteen pounds of grain to produce one pound of beef. That is not a good return. It also takes 2,400 gallons of water to produce one pound of meat. This system is clearly depleting our natural resources. The prevalence of meat in the modern diet has also led to the dramatic rise of degenerative illnesses like cancer and heart disease. Moreover, the animals themselves are increasingly unhealthy contributing to an unhealthy food supply.

We have a collision coming in the near future. That collision could take place on a global scale between population growth on one hand, and limited water, energy, and other natural resources on the other.

The trend lines all point to the exponential growth of a variety of negative factors that threaten human survival. Rain forest depletion, ozone depletion, the depletion of fish, and growth in the number of motor vehicles all are coming to a head. The word that describes all of these modern trends is "unsustainability." The modern way of life is clearly unsustainable.

What is inevitable if we do not change? Collapse of the entire planetary system, both natural and manmade.

What is our choice? Do we continue along the path of un-sustainability or do we change? What degree of change has to take place for us to pass through this crisis and enter an era of peace and prosperity? Just as we have seen these many negative trend lines converging, we have also seen a growing awareness of a sustainable way of life.

Opposite to the modern agricultural system, based on mono-cropping, artificial fertilizing, the application of pesticides, and the prevalence of GMOs, is a more sustainable organic trend that is growing throughout the world. Organic farmers are not using fertilizers and pesticides, but are rotating crops and using other sustainable practices.

As a part of that positive trend, farmers in New England have started growing organic rice, including in rice paddies. Several are producing it commercially. We never imagined that rice farming would succeed here due to the cold climate and short growing season. But apparently local farmers succeeded.

To get more information, Google "Vermont Rice." Also, in the Pioneer Valley, Christian Elwell has been growing rice for over thirty years first on dry land and recently in a rice paddy at his farm at South River Miso.

If you visit the South River web site (SouthRiver-Miso.com), you'll see colorful instructional photos and videos of each stage of the rice cycle. You'll see planting in the spring, the flowering rice plants in the summer, and harvesting and threshing the rice in the fall. All of these steps are done the traditional way, on a small scale and by hand. Our hope is that these positive developments, however preliminary, eventually transform agriculture in the United States and throughout the world.

The organic trend is now going global. In his annual Parliamentary Address, Russian President Vladimir Putin stated his desire to see Russia become the world's leading exporter of organic food.

Rice harvest at South River Miso

According to an article by Bryan MacDonald entitled, "Putin wants Russia to become world's organic super-power..." published online at rt.com:

> "However, for this writer, the most notable element of Putin's speech was when he turned his attention to agriculture. Readers who have flown over Russia will have noticed the almost complete absence of intensive farming when compared with Europe or North America. The only real exception here is the southern Krasnodar region, which benefits from a very benign climate. There is little doubt that if Russia got its act together in

this regard, it could probably feed the whole planet.

"In the 21st century, Russian food production has improved. Now, Putin is proposing a major focus on the area. *'By 2020, Russia must provide itself with all food,"* he implored. *"We need to cultivate the millions of acres now idle.'*

"As the Kremlin has rejected the idea of GMO food production, now a mainstay of American agriculture, Russia could become the world's principal supplier of high-quality organic food. Meaning there is potential to dominate the *"high-end"* market in both the West and in other wealthy countries—like China and the Middle Eastern states. *'We are not only able to feed ourselves taking into account our lands, water resources – Russia is able to become the largest world supplier of healthy, ecologically clean and high-quality food which the Western producers have long lost, especially given the fact that demand for such products in the world market is steadily growing,'* said Putin."

We are now in the transition between an unsustainable centralized system and a sustainable distributed system. In Russia, up to 50% of food is produced by local dacha gardens and family farmers in a system of distributed agriculture. In America, the family farm was distributed and local. It was put out of business by giant highly centralized factory farms. American agriculture would be well advised to take a closer look at the Russian model.

The same thing has happened to merchandizing. There used to be locally owned businesses, such as clothing stores, hardware stores, and food stores, but these have been put out of business by Wal-Mart and other big box stores. The same trend has occurred in the natural food industry.

When I started macrobiotics in the 1970s, most natural food stores were locally owned. Now that industry has become increasingly centralized and corporate with the rise of Whole Foods and other national chains. We appreciate the convenience of Whole Foods, but there are advantages and disadvantages to that trend.

The key point in transitioning from an unsustainable, centralized civilization to a sustainable, distributed civilization is diet. The symbol of our modern unsustainable civilization is a diet based on meat and animal food, especially cattle, but also chicken, pigs, and other animals. This diet is highly inefficient and very low yield. A diet based on animal foods simply cannot support the world's growing population. A fresh, local, and organic plant based diet is the first step toward a sustainable civilization. Energy, economy, technology, politics, and other systems will follow the change in diet. The secret to whether humanity can pass through the modern crisis is whether or not humanity can make the transition from the modern diet to a more natural plant-based way of eating. To guide humanity through this crisis and into a new era of peace and prosperity is the deeper meaning of macrobiotics.

Edward Esko is vice president of Planetary Health, Inc. and founder of the International Macrobiotic Institute. He lives in the Berkshires.

BILL TARA
Cherishing Our Children's Future:
Realizing JFK's Dream
London, June 2018

"So, let us not be blind to our differences—but let us also direct attention to our common interest and to the means by which those differences can be resolved. And if we cannot end now our differences, at least we can help make the world safe for diversity. For, in the final analysis, our most basic common link is that we all inhabit this small planet. We all breathe the same air. We all cherish our children's future. And we are all mortal."
—John F. Kennedy

This speech by JFK has been sitting on my desktop for well over a month now. When Alex sent it to me and asked me to write few words about it I blithely agreed. Every so often I would re-read it and found myself saddened by these words.

My sadness was not prompted by the tragic death of a man who held such great promise, we all meet the fate of death. It was not by any sentimental attachment to the Kennedy mythology of Camelot; no political enterprise is without flaw. There is something deeper that was troubling me. This speech represents an intellect, civility, and compassion that is almost completely lacking in present day politics. Intellect, compassion and a vision of collective fairness have been overwhelmed by greed, nationalism and a hateful fear of the "other."

The dreams of the 60's and 70's of racial, religious, and gender equality are being eroded by repressed anger over changes that question our imagined past and collective ethics. As a student of the macrobiotic way of life, I must wonder if JFK and his excellent speechwriters would change their remarks to meet the challenges of today.

The Cold War is still in play now with the most insidious of weapons—the power of the Internet. The battle is, in many ways t he same, a fight for the hearts and minds of the many to serve the desires of the few. The diversity that JFK desired is now seen as a threat to imagined cultural purity. This combined with cultural agendas of the religious fanatics that populate powerful positions in major faiths and the increasing grip on the economy by the billionaire class is a formidable force to undermine democratic institutions.

As someone who has an abiding love of the environment and the health of all life on this small planet, Kennedy's statement that, "We all cherish our children's future" is called to question. It seems that we have lost the impulse to make life better for the next generation. We are eating the world and our hunger knows no end.

We know more than ever the dangers of environmental destruction, the toxic results of our food system and the suppression of the poor and yet put off any action that would imply changes in our daily "life style." The vision of peace that JFK referred to was peace for every nation and not just our own.

He knew that negativity was a sure formula for threats

and impulsive action. The lines, "...problems are man-made— therefore, they can be solved by man. And man can be as big as he wants," are particularly useful at this time. In the face of social and environmental destruction, we need to keep our focus on being "bigger" than the problems we have created. It is a call for macro and not micro solutions. As another famous social force of the time, Martin Luther King, said, "Now is not the time for incrementalism," now is the time for thinking big and speaking truth to power.

Bill Tara help found and direct the Community Health Foundation in London, the Kushi Institute in America, and is co-director of MacroVegan. He is the author of Macrobiotics and Human Behavior *and lives in London.*

JOHN LIEBMANN
Observing the UN Conference to Ban Nuclear Weapons and Implications for Peace
New York, June 2018

On a Friday evening in March 2017, The Unitarian Church of All Souls hosted a reception for international delegates and members of Civil Society who were in New York for a conference at the United Nations on nuclear disarmament. The first phase of deliberations had just completed and would resume in mid-June with the goal being the adoption of a legally binding treaty banning nuclear weapons.

I have been a member of the All Souls Nuclear Disarmament Task Force for more than a decade; service on the task force had helped me live out several of the denomination's guiding principles, namely "respect for the interdependent web of all existence, of which we a part" and "the goal of world community with peace, liberty and justice for all. " In the previous fall, two weeks before the presidential election of 2016, the task force co-sponsored a well-attended appearance by former Secretary of State, William Perry, in which he spoke of his concerns for the safety of the planet. (1) Perry described them as rivaling or surpassing concerns during the height of the Cold War. Then, six months later, the UN was holding a major conference on nuclear disarmament.

The mood of those at the reception was optimistic. Speakers from around the world expressed confidence that a solid start had been made by the more than 120 nations who were participating. They looked forward to returning to adopt a "legally binding instrument, leading to the total elimination" of nuclear weapons in the words of the bold title of the conference. I spoke with representatives from Japan, Brazil, France and Great Britain and when an opportunity was presented to me to observe the second session at the UN, I accepted with enthusiasm.

Despite having grown up in New York City I had not participated in a major event at the UN since a program for high school students in the early 1960's. In fact, the extent of my relationship with the scenic campus along the East River in recent years has been passing by on the First Avenue bus after work near the Brooklyn Bridge for New York City government. So, when I walked across the UN Plaza towards the General Assembly building, I was struck by the sweeping view of the river and an expanding Long Island City skyline in the background. In the foreground, at the southern tip of Roosevelt Island I noticed the new park, named for Franklin Roosevelt's "Four Freedoms" which he had described in a 1941 speech. One of those four was the freedom from fear.

I

The second session of the "United Nations conference to negotiate a legally binding instrument to prohibit nuclear weapons, leading towards their total elimination" was

headquartered in a large conference room in the base-
ment of the General Assembly building. In the front of the
room were desks for all the nation states; in the rear of
the hall were five rows reserved for representatives from
Civil Society. On each desk was a microphone and when a
speaker was recognized by the President of the Conference, Elayne Whyte Gomez from Costa Rica, that person's
microphone was activated allowing the conversation to
be heard through a headphone available at each desk.
Translation services were available in six languages
including English, Spanish and Chinese.

There was standing room only in the Civil Society
section when I entered on the morning of June 15, 2017
as deliberations resumed. The participants were consid-
ering the text of the Draft Convention on the Prohibition
of Nuclear Weapons which President Gomez and her staff
had prepared from the first round of negotiations. Nation
states were commenting about their hopes for the
conference.

I was waiting to be seated so that I could fully follow
the remarks; what was apparent from the start was which
nations were participating and which were not. Speakers
included representatives from Egypt, New Zealand, Cuba,
Malaysia, Nigeria and Iran among others. The desk for the
United States was situated several rows in front of the
section for Civil Society in the middle of the hall. It was
empty as were those for eight other nation states with
nuclear weapons including France, Great Britain and
China. Other European nations under the "nuclear
umbrella" of NATO were also missing; the only nation in
this category that was present was the Netherlands.
There were absences in this conference but there were
also more than 120 nations present at the UN, in action

on a subject that Secretary Perry had called one of two existential threats to our planet. How had this come to pass? Why now and why here?

II

The creation of the United Nations and the threat of nuclear weapons are linked in history. The organizing conference for the UN was held in San Francisco in late April 1945, less than two weeks after the death of President Roosevelt. In August 1945 President Truman, who succeeded Roosevelt, made the decision to drop atomic bombs on Hiroshima and Nagasaki, Japan which ended WWII but did not quell international concern about the consequences of the use of these weapons. On January 24, 1946 the first resolution of the UN General Assembly called for elimination of nuclear weapons; this statement is included in the Preamble of the final text of the ban treaty.

Almost 500 nuclear tests were conducted between 1945 and 1963 when the Partial Test Ban Treaty was signed. Concern grew about fallout from both underwater and atmospheric tests. In 1968 the Non-Proliferation Treaty (NPT) was adopted by most of the nations of the world; three nations who possess these weapons were not signatories. These are India, Pakistan and Israel. North Korea, which originally was a signatory in 1985, withdrew in 2003 after a nuclear detonation.

The NPT is premised on an agreement between nuclear-armed states like the United States and Russia and non-nuclear states. The latter states agree never to acquire nuclear weapons and the former states, in turn, agree to share nuclear energy technology and to pursue disarmament with the goal of elimination of nuclear arsenals. Article VI of the NPT provides: "Each of the Parties to the Treaty undertakes to pursue negotiations in good faith on effective measures relating to cessation of the nuclear arms race at an early date and to nuclear disarmament, and on a treaty in general and complete under strict and effective international control." This article has been central to disarmament efforts. There was an expectation about how the deliberations were to be conducted and a general statement about the timing of such deliberations. It also helped reinforce the obligation for disarmament on the part of signatories to the treaty.

The obligation to disarm was also recognized in an important advisory opinion regarding the legality of nuclear weapons. (2) After years of debate the UN General Assembly in 1994 asked the International Court of Justice in the Hague "whether the threat or use of nuclear weapons is permitted in any circumstance under international law." The advisory opinion, which was delivered on July 6, 1996, was mixed: on the one hand, the court recognized what it called the "overriding consideration of humanity which applies to the rules of law in armed conflict"..."Means and methods of warfare which do not include a distinction between civilian and military targets or which would result in unnecessary suffering to combatants are prohibited." On the other hand, the court said that it could not "lose sight of the fundamental right of every State to survival, and thus to its right to resort to self defense. Nor can it ignore the policy of deterrence".

This language indicated differences of opinion among the justices over what they described as "eminently difficult" legal issues posed by nuclear weapons. But In a show of unity all the justices restated the importance of Article VI of the NPT. The obligation for nuclear disarmament, they said, "remains without any doubt an objective of vital importance to the whole of the international community."

International pressures continued to grow, especially from among most of the world's non-nuclear states for expedited action to outlaw nuclear weapons. One focus was on the unacceptable and catastrophic humanitarian impact of any use of these weapons. Following a NPT Review Conference in 2010, three governmental meetings were held in 2013 and 2014 in Oslo, in Nayarit, Mexico and in Vienna on this subject. During this period mounting scientific evidence showed that even a limited nuclear war would cause unimaginable climate change leading to widespread famine that would potentially put billions of people at risk. (3)

It was the growing awareness of this "existential" risk to the planet that led to the 2016 UN Open Ended Working Group in Geneva, Switzerland which recommended that the UN convene a conference in New York to develop new legally binding measures, leading to the elimination of nuclear weapons. The message was that the time was now and not in some distant future. There was an obligation for disarmament established through international treaties and law. Even though some nations would absent themselves and the task was daunting, the consensus among a majority of UN member states was to proceed.

III

As I attended sessions of the conference in June and July 2017, I came to appreciate the hard work that goes into such a document. President Gomez and her staff had released the draft text before the resumption of deliberations. Here are a few of the major issues that were worked out during deliberations, sometimes involving heated debate:

The draft text opened with a lengthy Preamble which puts the document in historical and aspirational context. There were a series of statements to which the States Parties to the treaty agreed. In the final text a new first statement appeared in the Preamble: "Determined to contribute to the realization of the purposes and principles of the Charter of the United Nations." The link between the founding of the international organization and the issue of nuclear weapons was established immediately.

Another statement in the draft statement in the Preamble referred to deep concern "about the catastrophic humanitarian consequences...and the consequent need to make every effort to ensure that nuclear weapons are never used again under any circumstances." The conference reviewed this language to clarify its intent in the final text of the treaty. After describing deep concern for the consequences from any use of such weapons, the statement recognized the "need to completely eliminate such weapons, which remains the only way to guarantee that nuclear weapons are never used again under any circumstances."

There were several other noteworthy additions to the Preamble in the final text. One acknowledges the "ethical imperatives for nuclear disarmament... which is a global public good of the highest order, serving both national and collective security interests."

Another new statement referred to the "slow pace of nuclear disarmament, the continued reliance on nuclear weapons in military and security concepts, doctrines and policies and the waste of economic and human resources on programmes for the production, maintenance and modernization of nuclear weapons." The United States, even under President Obama, a supporter of disarmament in his speeches, has budgeted to spend hundreds of billions of dollars to "modernize" the nuclear arsenal.

One significant addition to Article I in the final text was a prohibition on not only the use of nuclear weapons but also on the threat to use them. The 1996 Advisory Opinion from the International Court of Justice made reference to the policy of deterrence that was central to Cold War thinking. These are different times and thinking has changed. John Burroughs, Executive Director of the Lawyers Committee on Nuclear Policy, wrote: "At its core nuclear deterrence is an ongoing threat of use of nuclear weapons should certain circumstances arise...it is a concrete, elaborated military posture, embodied in doctrines and deployments, and in infrastructure that supports deployed nuclear forces." The goal of eliminating these weapons is not possible if nuclear deterrence as a doctrine is not replaced and the wording of Article I was a step in that direction. (4)

In the final text of the treaty, Articles 6 and 7 reflected the thinking and advocacy of many nation states, especially those which have been impacted by the testing of nuclear weapons. The articles relate to victim assistance and environmental remediation in Article 6 and international cooperation in Article 7. In the draft text parties like the Marshall Islands or Algeria which have had testing occur in areas under their jurisdiction were held responsible for providing assistance, including "medical care, rehabilitation and psychological support... for social and economic inclusion." There was no mention of the responsibility of nation states that were conducting the tests or, in the worst case, exploding nuclear devices.

Many state parties were struck by the inherent unfairness; they wanted responsibility to extend to this latter group. Here is the final text of Article 7, Paragraph 6: "Without prejudice to any other duty or obligation that it may have under international law, a State Party that has used or tested nuclear weapons or any other nuclear explosives shall have a responsibility to provide adequate assistance to affected States Parties, for the purpose of victim assistance and environmental remediation." (5)

The Holy See also participated in the conference, strongly advocated for international cooperation in addressing the consequences of use or testing and suggested the establishment of a fund administered by the UN for these purposes. In this debate especially, the interests of indigenous peoples and of women and children, among other interests, were raised and recognized.

One other modification to the text that I found significant related to the conference's intent to be inclusive in future meetings. This extended to both nations that were not party to this treaty and to members of Civil Society including the International Committee of the Red Cross and international legal associations. The final language of Article 8, Paragraph 5 is affirmative in including these entities. In doing so conference participants were recognizing the invaluable contributions of Civil Society. They were also extending invitations to nuclear armed nations and those under a nuclear umbrella to participate in the future.

IV

On the morning of July 7, 2017 there was a packed house with standing room only when I arrived. On this last day of the conference a vote to approve the treaty had already been taken: the result was 122 nations in favor and one nation opposed. The Netherlands sided with other NATO countries who were not in attendance and voted against adopting the treaty. The rationale was that the NPT, and not this new one, was the primary legal instrument for disarmament. When the Dutch representative spoke, there was respectful silence.

But that was not the mood in the hall. After a standing ovation after the vote was taken, speakers captured what the moment meant. The Egyptian representative, for example, described "an extraordinary gathering for a more peaceful and secure world." Egypt was "proud to be among the community of nations who took this step." That was also the mood in the Civil Society section where many hugs were exchanged.

A short afternoon session closed the conference. Speaking for Civil Society, the Director of the International Committee of the Red Cross called the BAN treaty a turning point and a moment whose significance can't be overstated. The Red Cross promised to actively promote the treaty. Then, the UN Undersecretary for Disarmament Affairs spoke and called the treaty a "beacon of hope"; it would fill the legal gap. What remained was addressing what she called "the political gap".

The conference had been inspired, in part, by the suffering of Japanese citizens who were victims of atomic blasts in Hiroshima and Nagasaki. These people, the *hibakusha*, included Setsuko Thurlow, who attended the conference and who spoke forcefully about waiting more than decades for this moment. (6) About the treaty, she said that nuclear weapons have been immoral; now they are illegal.

Ms. Thurlow appeared in a picture with the Conference President, Ambassador Gomez, at the end of the conference. (7) It was both poignant and symbolic of high accomplishment. I was left with a sense of gratitude for having had the privilege to observe these proceedings. I was also energized in tackling the next steps.

There was the need for a strategy for reaching out to those states who chose not to participate including all those with nuclear arms. The conference was a bold action by a majority of nations in the UN. One observer counselled boldness and forthrightness in making the ethical case for disarmament. (7) Others pointed to the obligation for disarmament by all nations, whether they were signatories to this treaty or not. (8) The nuclear ban treaty promised to strengthen, not weaken, this obligation. This new legal instrument, when adopted by at least fifty member states, represented a "good faith" effort to live up to the requirements of Article VI of the Non-Proliferation Treaty.

ENDNOTE

It is one year since the second session of the UN Conference was convened. In the three weeks between June 15 and July 7 of 2017, diplomats from around the world and members of Civil Society worked together to review a draft treaty, negotiate its text and move it to final status. It was a special time, full of hope and promise, and last fall, a lead organizer of the UN Conference, the International Campaign to Abolish Nuclear Weapons (ICAN), was awarded the 2017 Nobel Peace Prize.

In 2018 a variety of strong international challenges have become evident. First, the leaders of the United States and North Korea, after insulting and threatening each other, agreed to meet in a face to face meeting in Singapore on June 12, 2018. The summit has been on again and off again. Unlike other meetings where the agenda is set and much of the diplomatic work has been accomplished, this meeting occurs without much preliminary groundwork.

The American administration also announced its intention to unilaterally withdraw from the Iran De-nuclearization Agreement. This is in violation of the terms of the agreement and is contrary to the advice of U.S. military, security experts and all our European allies. It also comes despite international certifications that Iran has been in compliance with the agreement.

Last year the UN Undersecretary for Disarmament Affairs distinguished a "political gap" that remained to be filled. That gap has grown wider in the past twelve months and much work remains to be done. What kind of work? The kind that an earlier American President spoke about in June, 1963.

It was President John F. Kennedy who delivered the Commencement Address at American University in Washington D.C. and devoted it to what he called "the most important topic on earth: peace." He had in mind "genuine peace... the kind of peace that makes life on earth worth living. " That was "not merely peace for Americans but peace for all men and women, not merely peace in our time but peace in all time." (9)

At the time of the speech I was completing my sophomore year in high school. JFK was a hero. He had challenged the American people to put a man on the moon before the end of the decade. When John Glenn was honored with a ticker tape parade down the Canyon of Heroes on Lower Broadway, I made a rare subway trip downtown to watch it. President Kennedy also spoke about other kinds of service, service to the country, and his administration made opportunities available internationally in the Peace Corps and domestically in Volunteers in Service to America (VISTA) and in other programs.

Kennedy spoke of peace in his speech in the aftermath of the Bay of Pigs invasion of Cuba and the subsequent Cuban Missile Crisis. In his first term the country had come close to a nuclear exchange with the Soviet Union. It led the young President to question if victory in the Cold War with the USSR was the goal if that meant being led to the brink. He questioned his advisors, some of whom were saying that it was useless to speak of "peace or world law or disarmament" until the Soviet Union adopts a more enlightened attitude. He hoped they would and suggested the United States could help.

But there was another task for Americans: "we must reexamine our own attitudes, as individuals and as a nation, for our attitude is as essential as theirs." Examine our attitudes towards peace, a task which, he suggested, many think is impossible. This often led to the conclusion that war is inevitable and that mankind is doomed. Kennedy did not accept this defeatist view and then outlined to the American University graduates a more nuanced view. He sought a peace "more practical, more attainable" based on "a series of concrete actions and effective agreements which are in the interests of all concerned." Genuine peace, he said, "must be the product of many nations, the sum of many acts."

He ended his dramatic speech making reference to his own WWII generation who "have already had enough—more than enough—of war and hatred and oppression." He pledged that the United States would do its part to build a world of peace "where the weak are safe and the strong are just." We are not helpless before that task, he said, nor hopeless of its success.

President Kennedy would not get to implement this strategy or to deal with a conflict in Southeast Asia that was starting to expand; in a matter of months he was gunned down in Dallas. One interpretation of those events is that at the height of the Cold War, he chose a new direction for the country and paid the ultimate price for his bold vision and courage. (10) Making peace with our adversaries without resorting to war was a radical stand. It offended some with interests in the growing complex of military, corporate and intelligence interests that Dwight Eisenhower had identified as a threat in his farewell speech as President.

John Kennedy's 1963 speech resonates with current events today. He was willing to think globally and to focus not only on our adversaries but also on ourselves, on what he called the "dedication of our own lives." He also sought to strengthen the UN: to develop it so that it could "resolve disputes on the basis of law...and "create conditions under which arms can finally be abolished."

In closing a "political gap" that stands between us and a breakthrough in implementing new international agreements such as the BAN treaty, we need to draw inspiration from the words of a prescient American President and world leader. We also would be well advised not to underestimate the forces that stand in opposition to human progress through disarmament and peace. How should one approach these challenges? "Confident and unafraid, we must labor on − not towards a strategy of annihilation but towards a strategy of peace."

Where does that leave the current negotiations between North Korea and the United States? Certainly, the Singapore meeting was an important first step away from overheated rhetoric and towards diplomacy, a symbolic act that one expert has called the "most promising feasible path available at this point."(11) Secretary of State Mike Pompeo will be the leader of the American team negotiating denuclearization with North Korea. He will be dealing with an adversary that over several generations has not kept its word and has withdrawn from international agreements. The issues are highly technical and complicated.

This is a great challenge that previous administrations have not been able to conclude. Secretary Pompeo would be well advised to assemble a top flight team and review the history of past negotiations. (12) I hope he is also able to make some time to examine his own attitude towards peace. In so doing he may come to believe that the path towards peace requires full partners that include South Korea, among others. The stakes are high and there is the opportunity for our leaders to rise to the occasion.

NOTES

1. Go to the Perry Project online to watch a video of Secretary Perry's speech at the Unitarian Church of All Souls in October 2016;

2. See "Looking Back: The 1996 Advisory Opinion of the International Court of Justice", by John Burroughs, in *Arms Control Today*, July/August 2016, pp. 32-36;

3. See "An Open Letter to President-Elect Trump about Nuclear Weapons and Nuclear Winter" by Rutgers Professor Alan Robock, in the *Bulletin of the Atomic Scientists*, November 11, 2016;

4. See *Reaching Critical Will, Nuclear Ban Daily*, June 21st edition of the UN Conference newsletter for discussion of threats. (The photograph of Conference President Elayne Whyte Gomez and atomic bomb survivor Setsuko Thurlow at the close of proceedings can be found in the July 8th edition of Reaching Critical Will, p.6);

5. In April 2014 Tony de Brum led a delegation from the Republic of the Marshall Islands and an international legal team in filing complaints against all nine nuclear armed states in the International Court of Justice, claiming that obligations under international law to disarm were not being fulfilled. The court narrowly dismissed the cases on procedural grounds but attention had been drawn to the slow pace of disarmament negotiations. Mr. de Brum was a boy in 1954 when he witnessed a powerful nuclear test explosion over the Bikini Atoll, part of the Marshall Islands. He dedicated his life to the causes of nuclear disarmament and protection of the environment. Mr. De Brum passed away on August 21, 2017.

6. I lived for several years in Brookline, Massachusetts in the early 1980's which was a center of macrobiotic studies at that time; I shopped at a natural foods grocery and ate at a health food restaurant there. This was also the home of Aveline and Michio Kushi who migrated from Japan in 1949 to the United States. Both had been students of George Ohsawa in Japan. Ohsawa made the connection between food and health and then health and peace, the latter a subject of concern to Michio Kushi who had studied politics and law at the University of Tokyo. The Kushis subsequently moved their base of operations to the Berkshires where I participated in programs over the years. I have benefitted personally from learning about food and following lifestyle suggestions. In a larger sense, I have been inspired by their example. They came here in the aftermath of WWII to share lives committed to wholeness and peace.

7. See "After the Nuclear Weapons Ban Treaty: A New Disarmament Politics", by Zia Mian, in the *Bulletin of the Atomic Scientists*, July 7, 2016; and

8. See the "Lawyers Letter on the Abolition of Nuclear Weapons", published by the International Association of Lawyers Against Nuclear Weapons (IALANA) on June 23, 2017 at the United Nations. For a further discussion of these

issues including a review of the first session of the conference, see "Key Issues in Negotiations for a Nuclear Weapons Prohibition Treaty", by John Burroughs in *Arms Control Today*, June 2017, pp. 6-13.

9. James W. Douglass, in his 2008 book, *JFK and the Unspeakable: Why He Died and Why It Matters*, recounts the story of President Kennedy's turning from Cold War orthodoxy towards peacemaking with the enemy. Douglass, a Catholic scholar and peace activist, discusses the enormous stakes at play in a world with nuclear weapons. He recounts the trepidations of the Catholic monk and author, Thomas Merton, who feared that the United States during President Kennedy's term would launch a first strike on the Soviet Union. Merton believed that the young President needed a breakthrough in spiritual depth and empathy in order to avoid such a catastrophe. He needed to achieve a deeper level of "dedication" and the speech at American University was one example of JFK's journey of exploration in the last years of his life.

10. Douglass also discusses in some detail the forces aligned against an individual with great responsibility and power who turns away from official violence and war and "repents" or seeks peace. John Kennedy became President in an era of American ascendency and exceptionalism. Nuclear weapons were part of the era and some Cold War figures, particularly in the intelligence services, rationalized the use of anti-democratic and covert means to achieve what they believed were legitimate ends. President Kennedy challenged Cold War assumptions and replaced leading governmental officials.

11. Graham Allison commented on the Singapore meeting on the website of the Belfer Center for Science and International Affairs. The Belfer Center is part of the John F. Kennedy School of Government at Harvard University; Allison is the former Director of the Belfer Center and Douglas Dillon Professor of Government at Harvard.

12. Also commenting on the Belfer Center website was Wendy Sherman, Senior Fellow. During the Obama Administration, she served as Under Secretary of State for Political Affairs and was the lead negotiator on the Iran Nuclear Deal. During the Clinton administration she was Policy Coordinator for North Korea.

John Liebmann graduated from Brown University with a Bachelor's degree in American Civilization. He served as a VISTA Volunteer in the McCully and Moiliili neigborhoods of Honolulu and earned a Master's degree in Urban and Regional Planning from the University of Hawaii. After returning to the mainland, he served as a planner and administrator at the New York City Department of Housing Preservation and Development. He is a Vice Chair of the Nuclear Disarmament Task Force at the Unitarian Church of All Souls in New York City. He is also a longtime supporter of the Lawyers Committee on Nuclear Policy based at the United Nations.

DENNIS KUCINICH
Speech to the UN General Assembly Meeting on Disarmament
September 26, 2017

Your Excellency, President of the General Assembly, Distinguished Ministers, Delegates and Colleagues:

I speak on behalf of the Basel Peace Office, a coalition of international organizations dedicated to the elimination of nuclear weapons.

The world is in urgent need of truth and reconciliation over the existential threat of development of and use of nuclear weapons.

We have a shared global interest in nuclear disarmament and nuclear abolition, deriving from the irreducible human right to be free of contemplation of extinction.

This is the place and now is the time to take confidence-building measures, new diplomatic steps towards averting a nuclear catastrophe, to enact the new ban treaty, to refrain from precipitating nuclear showdowns, to begin anew the quest to eliminate nuclear weapons through reciprocal trust-building.

We from Civil Society insist upon structured, legally affirmed nuclear arms treaties compelling nonviolent conflict resolution, mindful of the founding principle of the United Nations to "end the scourge of war for all time."

Today's world is interdependent and interconnected. Human unity is the first truth.

Technology has created a global village. When a greeting can be sent to the other side of the world in a matter of seconds, this represents the constructive power of global citizens, affirming our commonality.

Contrast that with a nation sending an ICBM missile with a nuclear warhead.

There is a thin line between deterrence and provocation. An aggressive expression of nuclear sovereignty is illegal and suicidal.

The threat of the use of nuclear weapons nullifies our humanity.

Let us hear and heed the demands for peace and nonviolent conflict resolution from the peoples of the world community.

Let the nations of the world affirm the evolutionary potential of technology for peace. This great institution cannot do it alone.

Each one of us must disarm and abolish any destructive force in our own lives, our own homes and our own communities which breed domestic violence, spousal abuse, child abuse, gun violence, racial violence.

The power to do this is in the human heart, where courage and compassion reside, where the transformative power, the conscious willingness to challenge violence anywhere helps to tame that beast everywhere.

If we are to eliminate nuclear weapons, we must also eliminate destructive rhetoric.

Here we acknowledge the power of the spoken word. Words create worlds. Harsh words, the exchange of threats between leaders, begins a dialectic of conflict, breeding suspicion, fear, reaction, miscalculation and disaster. Words of mass destruction can unleash weapons of mass destruction.

The ghosts from Nagasaki and Hiroshima hover over us today, warning us that time is an illusion, that the past, the present and the future are one and can be obliterated in a flash, proving nuclear weapons are a fact of death, not life.

Nations must explicitly abandon designs for empire and nuclear dominance.

The brandishing of nuclear weapons triggers the inevitability of their use.

In the name of all humanity, this must stop.

Instead of new nuclear nations and a new nuclear architecture, we need new, clear action to create a world with freedom from fear, freedom from violent expression, freedom from extinction, and a legal framework to match.

On behalf of the Basel Peace Office and Civil Society, we say let peace be sovereign. Let diplomacy be sovereign. Let hope be sovereign, through your work and our work.

Then we shall fulfill the prophecy that "nation shall not take up sword against nation."

We must save our world from destruction. We must act with a sense of urgency. We must destroy these weapons before they destroy us. A nuclear weapons-free world is waiting to be courageously called forth. Thank you.

Dennis Kucinich served 16 years in the U.S. Congress and was mayor of Cleveland, Ohio. He has twice been a candidate for president of the United States. He is a recipient of the Gandhi Peace Award. He is the sponsor of the Department of Peace, a Cabinet-level department that would seek to prevent war, promote diplomacy, and engage in dietary and nutritional education.

ALEX JACK

Beating Missiles into Tractors & Armies into Peace Corps
Oberlin, Ohio, November 1963 & the Berkshires, June 2018

Where Were You on November 22, 1963?

I was walking back to my dorm at Oberlin College from a political science class when I heard that President Kennedy had been shot. At first, it didn't register, but a few minutes later I found everyone glued—in shock and disbelief—to a TV in the common room watching the tragic events in Dallas unfold.

The next morning, my roommate Blake and I left for Washington DC to join in the mourning. We crashed at a dorm at George Washington University and added our thoughts and prayers to those of many others. Kennedy's shocking death moved me to write an essay on his legacy. In my tribute, "Beyond the Shot Heard Round the World," I observed:

> Though a historian and politician by profession, Kennedy always had both eyes on the future—and both eyes always open. Herein lay his greatness. With the slightest thaw in the national

or international deadlock, he could say with the conviction of a Martin Luther King, "I have a vision, I have a vision." Yet is his own words, he did not "claim the psalmist's an abundance of peace so long as the moon endureth."

While president, he understood and repeatedly made clear that there is but one reality that determines the ultimate future of all other realities and that reality can be expressed in the simple language of a chemical formula: $E=mc2$. And how it was expressed one never-to-be-forgotten October Day [the Cuban Missile Crisis], he knew better than any one living or dead.

Kennedy was a man who could agree with Emerson that the "march of civilization is a train of felonies," and talk and plan seriously of beating Cruise missiles into tractors and armies into peace corps.

He knew history well: That were it not for the optimistic messages of the Jesuses, Jeffersons, and Gandhis, ours would be a heritage entirely of high crimes and misdemeanors—that ours is also one of hope and the "vindication of right."

But he also knew the presidency demands political realism, and the White House is often an embassy for utopians-in-exile. As president, Kennedy looked, not only for the best of all possible solutions, but for acceptable alternatives as well.

Kennedy will be remembered for making crucial decisions always looking forward, not backwards, for emphasizing the positive, though accepting the negative, for rejecting Pandora's ghost and the theory of spontaneous ideological combustion, and most of all, for giving humanity the benefit of the doubt, not inhumanity.

On the tangible side, in the short span of his administration, his steps towards a world governed by law, for and of and by all peoples, were stumbles, certainly not strides. But he believed a series of stumbles could equal a stride, and if subsequent measures to the Test Ban Treaty and the wheat deal and the strengthening of the United Nations could be attained, the long day's journey into economic, political, and nuclear nightmare would end.

This was John Kennedy's hope, and he embarked on this crusade confidently—if not so courageously as some would have wished. But with his tragic end behind us, and his inspired pilgrimage before us, it is enough that he was the first American statesman to set out to take the 21st century by surprise, and not let it surprise us.

A scarce month before his death, he insisted: "If the worst should occur, and anyone survives [World War III] and ask the awful question, 'How did it happen?' he must not receive the incredible reply, 'Ah, if one only knew.'"

John Kennedy gave his life that that question never be asked. John Kennedy resolved that this and all generations to come be the "masters, not the victims, of their history." John Kennedy died a true master of history, to the bullet of a mere maker of history.

With his death, it was said "a great tree in the forest of humanity has fallen and a star of flesh and blood has faded." But from scorched trees, other timbers spring, and of what stuff are stars made but from other stars?

John Kennedy was life that willed to live in the midst of life that willed not to live. John Kennedy was reason that yearned to reason in the midst of irreason. John Kennedy was hope that clung to hope in the midst of hopelessness.

My father, Homer, a Unitarian minister and social activist, was serving as executive director of SANE, the peace and disarmament group, during Kennedy's presidency. With Norman Cousins, editor of *Saturday Review*, Dr. Benjamin Spock, and other luminaries, he orchestrated nation wide public relations campaign and demonstrations to ban nuclear testing. The partial Test-Ban Treaty signed in the summer of 1963 by America, the Soviet Union, and UK (and eventually 123 other countries) was midwifed by Cousins. Through back-door diplomacy, he was instrumental in bringing Soviet Premier Khrushchev on board and suggested to JFK that he compose his historic peace speech to sway Congress and public opinion in the first major thaw in the Cold War.

Change in Course
JFK's death changed the direction of American history, especially the war in Vietnam, as James W. Douglass documents convincingly in his book *JFK and the Unspeakable: Why He Died and Why It Matters* (Touchstone, 2008). Like so many people in my generation, my life was also turned upside down as Lyndon Johnson, the new president, intensified America's involvement in Southeast Asia.

In 1967, I went to Vietnam as a reporter for the *Oberlin Review*, the school newspaper, and a syndicate of other college, university, and small town newspapers. The experience, especially an interview with Thich Tri Quang, the spiritual leader of Vietnam, changed my life. The Zen master told me that the destruction of the rice fields in the country—and loss of principal food—was as catastrophic as the threat of nuclear war. Upon returning home to Boston, I gravitated to macrobiotics and several years later started studying with Michio Kushi, who had the same perspective.

As a student, and later a teacher, of macrobiotics, I began to understand more deeply the biological and spiritual roots of war and peace. With Michio Kushi, I wrote *One Peaceful World*, a book on humanity's imperishable dream of a healthy, peaceful world. In the Far East, the ideogram for peace, pronounced *Wa*, is made of characters for "grain" and "mouth." By eating whole grains as the foundation of our diet, we create physical health and vitality, a sound mind, and clear judgment. Isaiah's injunction to "beat swords into plowshares and spears into pruning hooks" glances at a similar transformation of weapons of war into peaceful farming tools to grow barley, wheat, and other grains. In ancient Egyptian hieroglyphs, *aam*, the word of eating, is made of pictographs that mean "that which gives knowledge." Egypt's original name *Khemet* means "soul of the earth," or "land of wheat and barley."

In *One Peaceful World*, we included an account of macrobiotic peace promoters around the world. These included teachers in Lebanon who brought together warring Christians and Moslems by reintroducing Wise Bread, the traditional whole grain loaf that had been displaced by modern, highly processed fare. In Colombia, oppressed factory workers started preparing macrobiotic foods, improved the health and vitality of the community, and peacefully secured major social changes. In Portugal, macrobiotic food was introduced to prisoners in a maximum security prison and transformed the lives of several high-profile terrorists and gang leaders. One went on to study at the Kushi Institute and start a successful tofu and tempeh company.

In the Soviet Union, two medical doctors created Longevity, a macrobiotic healing center, in their hospital in Chelyabinsk, center for the country's nuclear weapons production. They helped many patients recover from leukemia, lymphoma, and throat cancer who had been exposed to radiation. In Syria, Baydaa Lylaa, a young Syrian graduate of Kushi Institute, returned to her war-torn country to give cooking classes. Through their nonprofit Fortunate Blessings Foundation, Bill and Joan began an international relief program to assist children in Indonesia, Sri Lanka, Nepal, Japan, and elsewhere, who had been traumatized from natural disasters, war, torture, and other misfortune. In Washington, D.C., Dennis Kucinich, a Congressman from Ohio, healed himself of Crohn's disease and went on to head the Peace Caucus on Capitol Hill and sponsor legislation to create a Department of Peace and protect the food supply from GMOs.

Camelot Revisited

In the summer of 1963, macrobiotic educator George Ohsawa (Michio and Aveline's teacher) visited New York and gave lectures diagnosing JFK's facial features. He explained that JFK was *sanpaku*—or showing whites under three sides of his eyes—a traditional diagnostic sign of nervous exhaustion. A person with such an energy field easily loses balance and presence of mind in the face of approaching danger and often suffers a serious, or even fatal, accident or misfortune. An article by Tom Wolfe in the *New York Herald-Tribune* reported that Ohsawa warned that the president's life was in imminent danger and could be assassinated. Unfortunately, Ohsawa was unable to reach Kennedy and avert the tragedy.

In *Camelot Revisited* (One Peaceful World Press, 1996), I penned an alternative history of what would have happened if President Kennedy had lived. The novel foretold the peaceful end of the conflict in Vietnam. But it projected a long, interminable war in Central America under the following Rockefeller Administration. As the Cold War heated up, the Soviets won the race to the moon and Chairman Mao made a triumphant visit to America. Eventually, New Camelot, the utopian 51st state, founded in the American heartland, led by Secretary of Health Michio Kushi, Secretary of Energy Karen Silkwood, Secretary of Music John Lennon, and Secretary of Poetry Gary Snyder, came into existence. The chaos of the late 20th century gradually subsided as macrobiotic values spread around the world.

There are many real "what if's" and "if only's." Judy MacKenney, a Massachusetts homemaker with stage 4 Lymphoma, recovered from a terminal prognosis with the help of macrobiotics, while Jacquie Kennedy Onnasis died of the same affliction. Judy went on to become a counselor and teacher and guide countless others to recover from cancer and other chronic disorders.

A Serious Threat

In today's era, the forces of nativism, racism, and authoritarianism are on the rise. In comparison with contemporary politicians in America, Europe, the Middle East, and Asia, most world leaders over the last generation were relatively sane. The degree of chaos and uncertainty in the world has risen in step with global warming, climate change, and other threats to the environment.

The outbreak of a new Cold War, the proliferation of nuclear states, and development of weapons of mass destruction by terrorist networks imperil modern society and the future of our species. Putting into practice "the Strategy of Peace" introduced in John F. Kennedy's American University Speech is more urgent than ever.

Alex Jack is president of Planetary Health, Inc. and author of One Peaceful World (with Michio Kushi), the One Peaceful World Cookbook (with Sachi Kato), and The Circle of the Dance: Achilles's Shield, Odysseus's Oar, Calypso's Axe, and the New Golden Age. He lives in the Berkshires.

APPENDIX
Declaration of Planetary Commonwealth

Preamble

"As the current Spiral of History ends in the early twenty-first century, a new spiral will form that will last for about the next twelve to thirteen thousand years. This new era has already begun to unfold as the old era draws to a close. The relationship of these two spirals is similar to an Olympic relay race in which two runners run in parallel for a brief distance until the baton is safely passed. When a secure hold is established, the new runner accelerates and takes off on his or her lap while the old runner fades away. In the human race—the contest to preserve and develop our natural biological quality and spirit—this period of overlap extend from roughly 1980 to 2100, when the Pole Star arrives directly overhead. The two spirals will proceed in parallel for a while until the new orientation is strong enough to lead and the old orientation decays. Realistically, it may take the momentum of the past disharmonious factors two or three generations to fade away.

"Thus although worldwide modern civilization will continue to decline and fall over the next several decades, humanity need not necessarily disappear. At the same time that biotechnology is developing, a new orientation of civilization will arise among those people who have individually reoriented their way of life according to the laws of nature and the Order of the Universe. Through their understanding and efforts, the construction of a new healthy and peaceful world will begin, by the unification of all antagonistic factors in human affairs.

"As the new orientation spreads, existing political, economic, ideological, and cultural systems will be seen as complementary to one another and will be allowed to evolve naturally as civilization as a whole develops a more peaceful direction. The safe start of this new age will be signaled by the establishment of a world federal government or planetary commonwealth to oversee the final abolition of nuclear weapons, to preserve the earth's natural resources and wildlife, and to facilitate the biological, psychological, and spiritual health and happiness of humanity. The arrival of Polaris, the North Star, directly overhead in about 2100, will mark the safe entry into the new Era of Humanity and the beginning of a new cycle of peace and unity that can be expected to last for many thousands of years as the celestial influence of the Milky Way increases."

—Michio Kushi and Alex Jack, *One Peaceful World*, St. Martin's Press

Declaration of Planetary Commonwealth

We, the undersigned, on behalf of all people, all species, and the planet itself, hereby establish a Planetary Commonwealth. Planetary Commonwealth shall encompass all citizens of Earth, and represent and serve them, together with all species, and our natural environment on Earth. As founding members of Planetary Commonwealth, we hold these truths to be self-evident:

There is but One Universe. All men and women, all other species, and the planet itself originate within the infinite universe. All are manifestations of the infinite universe and all eventually return to the infinite universe. Thus, all men and women, all other species, and the planet itself share a common origin, a common existence, and a common destiny. As manifestations of the infinite universe, all men and women, all other species, and the planet itself possess independent sovereignty and self-regulating freedom. All human beings are infinitely free and absolutely sovereign.

Planetary Commonwealth exists within the infinite universe. Everything changes. The law of change is permanent and universal. The law of change is the law of peace, the law of harmony, and the law of love. The law of change is the one great law before which all other laws are relative and ephemeral. The law of change is the law of infinity. The law of change is the transcendent and universal law recognized by Planetary Commonwealth.

There is but One Planet. The earth is a singular undivided space, existing in time, under heaven, indivisible and shared by all. The earth consists of rivers and mountains, forests and deserts, oceans and land, valleys and plains. The only "boundaries" that exist are those created by nature, such as mountains, rivers, oceans, and deserts, and these are fluid not rigid. Human boundaries are artificial, produced not by nature, but by conceptual thought. We share our planetary environment with countless other species. Our destiny is their destiny. Their destiny is our destiny. Planetary Commonwealth shall represent all beings and all species. The earth is the one sovereign territory recognized by Planetary Commonwealth. On behalf of all species, we hereby declare the earth to be our sole sovereign territory. With the infinite universe as our witness, we vow to preserve, protect, cherish, and enjoy our planetary home.

There is but One People. We share a common origin in the infinite universe. We share a common existence that encompasses birth, growth, change, death, and rebirth. We share a common destiny to return to the infinite universe. We are all the brothers and sisters, parents and children, husbands and wives, lovers and friends, neighbors and passersby of one infinite universe. We have descended from common ancestors and spread over the entire planet with an endless range of diversity. We have within ourselves the ability to realize endless health, peace, prosperity, and freedom on the earth, without outside intervention or assistance. Differences are minor in comparison to the things we all share.

In solemn yet joyful recognition of the above, we, the undersigned, hereby affirm the truth of One Universe, One Planet, and One People. We, the undersigned, hereby establish Planetary Commonwealth upon these self-evident truths. By our signature, we declare ourselves to be founders and citizens of Planetary Commonwealth.

Amendments to the Declaration

Planetary Commonwealth shall secure for all people and all species a clean natural environment, including clean air and water; safe, healthful, and nutritious food; adequate shelter; and basic education for life, health, happiness, and peace. Planetary Commonwealth shall establish a territory without hunger, pollution, poverty, ignorance, homelessness, and war.

Planetary Commonwealth shall strive for world unity, peace, and understanding, while respecting, protecting, and preserving the endless diversity of all human beings and all other species. All citizens of Planet Earth, together with all the natural species inhabiting the territory, are members of and shareholders in Planetary Commonwealth. Planetary Commonwealth shall not discriminate according to age, race, sex, religion, economic status, political affiliation, species, health condition, dietary history, species profile, or level of education.

Planetary Commonwealth shall recognize that, together with clean air, water, soil, and light, humanity's health and happiness is influenced by the quality of food. Planetary Commonwealth shall encourage adoption of a plant-centered diet based on whole grains, beans, and fresh vegetables, together with locally produced organic produce and other products of local agriculture. Adoption of this dietary pattern shall serve as the foundation for sustainable personal health and prosperity. Organic and natural farming, cultivation, food production, and processing shall be the cornerstone of Planetary Commonwealth.

We, the undersigned, do hereby ratify the Declaration of Planetary Commonwealth. We hereby declare the establishment of Planetary Commonwealth upon the earth and invite all citizens to join as founding members.

www.ingramcontent.com/pod-product-compliance
Lightning Source LLC
Chambersburg PA
CBHW060803260726